Collins

Aiming for Level
Reading

3

Keith West

Series editor: Grant Westoby

William Collins' dream of knowledge for all began with the publication of his first book in 1819. A self-educated mill worker, he not only enriched millions of lives, but also founded a flourishing publishing house. Today, staying true to this spirit, Collins books are packed with inspiration, innovation and practical expertise. They place you at the centre of a world of possibility and give you exactly what you need to explore it.

Collins. Freedom to teach.

Published by Collins
An imprint of HarperCollins Publishers
77–85 Fulham Palace Road
Hammersmith
London
W6 8JB

Browse the complete Collins catalogue at
www.collinseducation.com

10 9 8 7 6 5 4 3 2 1
ISBN 978 0 00 731354 9

British Library Cataloguing in Publication Data.
A Catalogue record for this publication is available from the British Library.

Commissioned by Catherine Martin
Design and typesetting by Jordan Publishing Design
Cover Design by Angela English
Printed and bound by Martins the Printers

With thanks to Gemma Wain and Jo Kemp.

Acknowledgements

The publishers gratefully acknowledge the permission granted to reproduce the copyright material in this book. While every effort has been made to trace and contact copyright holders, where this has not been possible the publishers will be pleased to make the necessary arrangements at the first opportunity.

Extracts from *Mr Gum* and the *Biscuit Billionaire* by Andy Stanton, published by Egmont Books Ltd. (pp12,16); extract from *Dark Detective* by J.A.C. West, published by Badger Publishing (p52); extract from *Spook Manor* by David Orme, published by Badger Publishing (p52); extract from 'The Sailor' by Michael Owen, from *Spell Poems*, published by Weld Educational Books (p61).

The publishers would like to thank the following for permission to reproduce pictures in these pages:

Adam Dodd/istockphoto (p6); Peter Close/istockphoto (p7t); Diane Diederich/istockphoto (p7b); Jim Arbogast/Getty Images (p8t); istockphoto (p8b); Jonathan Larsen/istockphoto (p9); Andrew Drysdale/Rex Features (p10t); Jim Kruger/istockphoto (p10b); Semenscu Bogdan/istockphoto (p11); Olivier Blondeau/istockphoto (p12); istockphoto (p13); Mark Evans/istockphoto (p19); Terry Morris/istockphoto (p20t); Frances Twitty/istockphoto (p20b); istockphoto (p21t); Steven Hayes/istockphoto (p21b); Emilia Stasiak/istockphoto (pp25l, 25r); istockphoto (p26); John Bell/istockphoto (p28); istockphoto (p29); Betsy Dupris/istockphoto (p32); John Pitcher/istockphoto (pp34, 35); istockphoto (p36); Daniel Bobrowsky/istockphoto (p37); Action Press/Rex Features (p40); Ken McKay/Rex Features (p41); Dion van Huyssteen/istockphoto (p42); istockphoto (p46t); Ian Peters/istockphoto (p46b); Terry Healy/istockphoto (p47); Steve Luker/istockphoto (p48t); Stephen Patterson/istockphoto (p48b); Shaun Lowe/istockphoto (p52t); Nina Matthews/istockphoto (p52b); Susan Trigg/istockphoto (p53); istockphoto (p54); Lee Pettet/istockphoto (p57); istockphoto (60t); George Pchemyam/istockphoto (60b); Rebecca Ellis/istockphoto (61); Claudia Dewald/istockphoto (p62t); Chris Schmidt/istockphoto (p62b); istockphoto (p63).

Contents

Chapter 1

AF1 Use a range of strategies, including accurate decoding of text, to read for meaning

This chapter is going to show you how to

- Understand stories
- Understand a problem page
- Read and understand a poem.

What's it all about?

You will be able to read with understanding and expression.

Getting you thinking

Listen to your teacher read the story and spot words you do not know.

The Cool Gang

They all wore the same jackets. Their jackets were black. I could not see their faces. I did not know any of them. They all wore their hoods. They were the cool gang. People talked about them at school. They were tough. They did things at night. They broke into shops. They stole money. I knew they would get caught. Yes, one day they would get caught.

How does it work?

You will need to read the story to yourself several times and check how to pronounce words you are unsure of.

Now you try it

In groups, read the story. You might choose to share the reading and read one sentence each.

Development activity APP

Copy the following four sentences into your books and complete the sentences.

1 What colour were the boys' jackets?

The jackets were…

2 What was the gang called?

The gang was called the…

3 What does the writer think will happen to them?

The writer thinks the gang will…

Look at the story again.

Copy out the sentences that you know are true.

1 The gang leader was called Jake.
2 People talked about the gang at school.
3 The gang stole money.
4 The gang lived in Leeds.
5 One day they would get caught.
6 The gang carried guns.

Getting you thinking

You may have read the 'Problem Page' in magazines. Here are some problems that people are worried about.

Worried about anything? Write to Misha and she'll help. Sorted!

1 Dear Misha,

My best friend and I have fallen out. She's now best friends with other girls in my class. They've listened to the lies my ex-best friend has told them about me. Now they bully me. They text me with messages such as 'Get lost, nerd' and, 'We spread rumours'. They email me horrible messages. Sometimes, I feel life isn't worth living. What can I do? Please help me.

Jolene

2 Dear Misha,

I'm a victim of 'happy-slapping'. It mostly happens inside school. A gang of older boys tease and bully me. Then one of them pushes and hits me and the whole thing is recorded on a mobile phone. They all laugh and say they're going to put it on the internet. What can I do?

Graham

3 Dear Misha,

My mum has found a new boyfriend. He's good to Mum and my younger brother, but I don't think he likes me. I think it's my fault because I was jealous when he first came to my home. I used to help Mum but now she never wants my help. She just wants to spend all her time with him. What can I do?

Jessica

Here is a reply:

Dear…

You cannot accept what is happening to you. If all these things happen in school then talk to a teacher you can trust. If the text messaging does not stop, contact Childline. Someone there will help you – there are laws about cyber bullying to help too.

Misha

How does it work?

When you read the reply, you should be able to work out which of the three problems Misha is replying to.

Check your progress

LEVEL 2 I can write a simple reply to a problem

LEVEL 3 I can write a reply to a problem

Getting you thinking

Listen to your teacher read this poem to you.

Dad, you're not funny!

A few of my mates
Come around to our place,
And you're at the door
With that grin on your face.
You know that I know
You're a really good bloke,
But I'll curl up and die
If you tell us a joke!

We don't want to hear
About your days at school,
We don't want to watch
You try to be cool.
We don't want to know
How the world used to be.
We don't want to see
Those videos of me!

We don't want to laugh
At your riddles and rhymes,
At **musty** old tales
We've heard fifty times.
We don't want a quiz
Where we have to compete,
We don't want to guess
Why the hen crossed the street.

Please don't perform
That ridiculous dance
Like you did on the night
We went out to France.
Don't do impressions
Of pop stars on drugs.
Whatever you do
Don't swamp me with hugs!

So Dad, don't come in,
Your jokes are so dated
I often pretend
That we're not related.
I'd pay you to hide
If I had my own money,
The simple truth is –
Dad, you're not funny!

By Steve Turner

How does it work?

The poem is about how embarrassing dads can be.

Now you try it

In groups, read the poem to each other.
You might choose to share the reading and
read one verse each.

Development activity APP

1 Working in groups, work out how his dad is
   embarrassing in the first verse.

2 For written answers:

   a In the second verse, what four things is
      the boy worried that his dad might do?

      The boy is worried that his dad might…

   b In verse three, what four things is the boy
      worried that his dad might do?

      The boy is worried that his dad might…

   c What did dad do on the way to France?

      On the way to France…

   d In the last verse, what is the boy telling his dad?

      In the last verse, the boy is telling his dad…

e Why do you think the boy would pay his dad to hide?

The boy would pay his dad to hide because…

3 **Words I don't know**

Reread the poem and list all the words you don't know.

These might include the following:

curl

riddles

rhymes

compete

ridiculous

impressions

swamp

dated

related

Look at the poem again and try to work out the meaning of these words. If you still don't understand the words, look them up in a school dictionary.

Level Booster

LEVEL 2

- I can read a sentence with expression
- I can understand poems
- I can read a simple problem page

LEVEL 3

- I can write simple answers to questions about stories
- I can write simple answers to questions about poems
- I can read with increasing understanding and expression

LEVEL 4

- I can read with good understanding and expression
- I can write a reply to a problem page
- I can understand and comprehend a poem

Chapter 2

AF2 Understand, describe, select or retrieve information, events or ideas from texts and use quotation and reference to text

This chapter is going to show you how to

- Look at characters in non-fiction
- Make decisions about characters
- Look at characters in fiction.

What's it all about?

You will be able to understand texts.

Non-fiction means that the characters in the book really lived and the events in the book really happened. Your teacher will read the passage below.

Melbourne, Australia, 1860

In those days nobody knew what was in the middle of Australia. There might be a great lake or unknown cities. There might be more strange animals to find. Somebody had to explore Australia by walking from the South to the North. This man was Robert Burke.

Burke was born in Ireland. He was in the army there and then he joined the police. Later, he left Ireland and moved to a city called Melbourne, in Australia. He became a policeman there.

Burke liked police work. But sometimes it was boring. He wanted to do more with his life. Exploring Australia might bring him fame and fortune.

But there was a problem. Exploring a new country takes a lot of skill. You have to be ready when things go wrong. You have to have a plan. You have to know what to take and what to leave behind. Burke had never explored anywhere before. He knew nothing about leading a team.

How does it work?

In this short extract, we learn quite a few things about Robert Burke.

Now you try it

All about Robert Burke

1   Where was Burke born?
    He was born in…

2   What was Burke's first job?
    His first job was…

3   What was Burke's second job?
    His second job was…

4 What didn't Burke like about his second job?

He thought his second job…

5 What did Burke want to do with his life?

Burke wanted to…

6 Why was Burke not the best choice for the task?

Burke was not the best choice for the task because…

Development activity **APP**

More about Robert Burke

He made mistakes. The group began to make good progress. But the land was as dry as a bone. Another explorer, Wills, was worried they'd run out of water. But Burke was in too much of a rush to worry. He didn't even stop at water holes. It might slow him down.

If they spotted one in the afternoon he'd just pass by. He made his team march 16 hours a day. It didn't matter how thirsty they got.

But in the end even Burke had to stop for water. They'd reached some mountains. Between the mountains were deep valleys. In the valleys were dark pools of good water. They filled their water bags. If they hadn't come across the pools, they'd have died of thirst.

1   In groups, jot down the mistakes you think Burke makes. Work out why you think the explorers were lucky.

2   Hot seating: Hot-seat Robert Burke and ask him questions about his leadership.

Questions you could use:

- Why did you think you would make a good explorer?

- What have you done in the past to make you a good team leader?

- Why didn't you stop at water holes to allow the team to refill their water bags?

Check your progress

LEVEL 2   I can recognise a non-fiction text

LEVEL 3   I can understand a character's reasons for doing things

Getting you thinking

Four people arrive in your class at school.
Which one would you be friends with and why?

Jason Smart

Tall and thin. Full of fun but gets into trouble quickly. Tries to talk himself out of trouble. A known pickpocket, but never caught.

Dave Brading

Average height, a bit overweight. Quiet – likes to spend time on the computer. Is loyal to his friends, very reliable. Enjoys football – usually plays in goal.

Emma Harman

Blond, lively and talkative. Enjoys listening to hip hop. Has an eye for the boys but not very loyal. Silly in class.

Shelley Collit

Enjoys looking after small children and animals. Has two pet dogs. Likes to hang out with a small group of friends. Tries her best with school work.

How does it work?

You will need to read about each person before you can make a decision about whom you would be friends with.

Now you try it

Write a profile about yourself. You can set it out like the example below, if you wish.

Name: Shelley Collit

Date of birth: 10 April 1997

Family: Lives with mum, brother James (aged 14) and sister, Bethany (aged 8).

Personal details: Dark brown hair. Brown eyes. Average height.

Hobbies: Looking after two Jack Russell dogs. Listening to music. Looking after auntie's twin babies.

Likes: Reading fashion magazines, chilling out with friends. Eating chocolate.

Dislikes: Bullies.

Ambitions: To become a vet or to work with animals.

Greatest experience: Spending two weeks in Florida, visiting mum's stepsister.

Check your progress

| LEVEL 2 | I can form opinions about characters |
| LEVEL 3 | I can write a profile about myself |

Getting you thinking

This extract is from a story that is not true. The writer made the story up, which is why it is called fiction.

Mr Quinn was doing 'People We Admire' for Art. A huge boy with a freckly neck nominated Sir Alex Ferguson and listed all the trophies United had won. A boy called Jake said players were more important than managers and nominated Wayne Rooney for individual flair. Mr Quinn was looking around the room. Football was not taking him where he wanted to go. I put my hand up. He asked a girl.

'Don't know any footballers, sir.'

'It doesn't have to be a footballer.'

'Oh. Don't know, then, sir.'

I used my other hand to hoist my hand up higher.

'Damian, who do you admire?'

By now, most of the others were into players versus managers.

'I said, 'St Roch, sir.'

The others stopped talking.

'Who does he play for?'

'No one, sir. He's a saint.'

The others went back to football.

'He caught the plague and hid in the woods so he wouldn't infect anyone, and a dog came and fed him every day. Then he started to do miraculous cures and people came to see him – hundreds of people – in his hut in the woods. He was so worried about saying the wrong thing to someone that he didn't say a word for the last ten years of his life.'

'We could do with a few like him in this class. Thank you, Damian.'

'He's the patron saint of plague, cholera and skin complaints. While alive, he performed many wonders.'

'Well, you learn something new.'

He was looking for someone else now, but I was enjoying being excellent. Catherine of Alexandria came to mind. 'They wanted her to marry a king, but she said she was married to Christ. So they tried to crush her on a big wooden wheel, but it shattered into a thousand splinters – huge sharp splinters – which flew into the crowd, killing and blinding many bystanders.'

By Frank Cottrell Boyce

How does it work?

The author has shown us that Damian is different from the other boys in the class. The other boys are more interested in football. Damian is talking about saints, which does not interest anyone else. Even the teacher tries to change the subject.

Now you try it

Read the extract below and list five things you find out about Mr Gum's character.

Mr Gum was standing in front of the cracked mirror in the lonely bedroom of his old house getting ready to go out. He hated children, animals, fun and every cartoon ever made. What he liked was snoozing in bed all day. In fact, although it was eight o'clock in the evening, Mr Gum had only just got up! For not only was he a horror, he was a lazer too.

'You're up early, you handsome devil,' he said to his reflection. 'What do you fancy doin' today?'

'I fancies bein' even more evil than usual,' replied his reflection with a nasty laugh.

'Good idea, stupid,' said Mr Gum. 'In that case, I better look me most frightful.'

He got a felt-tip pen and drew some extra scowls on his forehead.

Then he scruffed up his big red beard to make it as wild and frightening as possible. It wasn't quite terrifying enough so he stuck a couple of beetles in it and a photo of a shark.

'That should do it,' he growled. Then he sproinged downstairs, jumped on a skateboard he'd nicked off a six-year-old, and headed into town.

By Andy Stanton

Development activity APP

a Jot down five things about your own character.

b Write five good things about the character of somebody you know well.

Check your progress

LEVEL 2   I can list five things about a character

LEVEL 3   I can write five things about a character I know well

Level Booster

LEVEL 2

- I can list five things about a character
- I can remember names of characters
- I can recognise a non-fiction text

LEVEL 3

- I can be a character in speaking and listening activities
- I can understand the main events in a text
- I can list things about a character

LEVEL 4

- I can write about a character using quotations
- I can write about events using quotations
- I can defend a character in speaking and listening activities

Chapter 3

AF3 Deduce, infer or interpret information, events or ideas from texts

This chapter is going to show you how to
- Understand characters' feelings
- Understand feelings through performance poetry
- Understand short poems.

What's it all about?

You will be able to see how writers allow characters to express their feelings.

Getting you thinking

Have you got a brother or sister? Do you get on with them?

Read this short poem.

Brother

Behaves like a maniac when grown-ups aren't watching

Rampages most when you want to be quiet!

Orders you around as if you were his servant

Thinks endlessly of fresh ways to torment you

Hates above everything to hear you admired

Eats with loud noises simply to irritate

Resorts to charm only as the last desperate bribe!

By Brian Merrick

How does it work?

The poet has thought of as many things as possible that a sister might dislike about her brother.

Now you try it

In groups, decide what the sister dislikes about her brother.

Development activity APP

Sister

Sweet as syrup whenever it suits her
Sour as old milk at all other times.

Is only good for messing things up, and
Interfering where she's absolutely no business.

Shows no brains, wit, or humour but always
Simpers like a moron when there's something she needs.

Teases and torments whenever you
Try to concentrate.

Exasperates all of your friends with her
Excruciating charm and smarminess.

Reduces anyone with sense to rage and frustration and is
Ridiculously over-rated by everyone but me!

By Brian Merrick

1 What does the brother think about his sister?

2 Find three things you think would particularly annoy the brother.

Getting you thinking

Listen to the poem as your teacher reads it to you.

Blenkinsop *by Gareth Owen*

'Late again, Blenkinsopp?
What's the excuse this time?'
'Not my fault, sir.'
'Whose fault is it then?'
'Grandma's sir.'
'Grandma's! What did she do?'
'She died, sir.'
'Died?'
'She's seriously dead all right, sir.'
'That makes four grandmothers this term,
    Blenkinsopp
And all on P.E. days.'
'I know. It's very upsetting, sir.'
'How many grandmothers have you got,
    Blenkinsopp?'
'Grandmothers, sir? None, sir.'
'You said you had four.'
'All dead, sir.'
'And what about yesterday, Blenkinsopp?'

'What about yesterday, sir?'
'You were absent yesterday.'
'That was the dentist, sir.'
'The dentist died?'
'No, sir. My teeth, sir.'
'You missed the maths test, Blenkinsopp!'
'I'd been looking forward to it, sir.'
'Right, line up for P.E.'
'Can't, sir.'
'No such word as "can't", Blenkinsopp.'
'No kit, sir.'
'Where is it?'
'Home, sir.'
'What's it doing at home?'
'Not ironed, sir.'
'Couldn't you iron it?'
'Can't, sir.'
'Why not?'
'Bad hand, sir.'
'Who usually does it?'
'Grandma, sir.'
'Why couldn't she do it?'
'Dead, sir.'

Check your progress

LEVEL 2   I can understand a performance poem

LEVEL 3   I can write a performance poem

How does it work?

This poem is meant to be read aloud.
Blenkinsopp's words are in italics *(italics)*.
This helps to show who is talking.

Now you try it

Working in pairs, one of you can be the
teacher; the other can be Blenkinsopp.
Read out the poem and, if possible, record it.

Play back or watch your performance to see if
you can improve your presentation.

Development activity APP

Imagine that Blenkinsopp is late home and his
tea is ruined. Working in pairs, one of you can
be his mum or dad and the other can be
Blenkinsopp, full of excuses. As Blenkinsopp is
at home, he will need a first name. Think of a
first name for Blenkinsopp before you write
your own performance poem.

Example:

'Late again, Adrian Blenkinsopp?

Your tea is ruined.

What's your excuse this time?'

'Sorry mum. It's not my fault.'

Getting you thinking

Read the poems. What do you think is happening in each poem?

R.I.P. Recipes

Here lies the body
Of Belinda Brewer:
Went for a swim
In the local sewer.

Here lies the body
Of Henry Hurst
Who stuffed himself with grub
Till his stomach burst.

Here lies the body
Of Percy Peat
Killed off by the stench
Of his own smelly feet.

Here lies the body
Of Wendy Wise.
She ate a mince pie
That was packed with flies.

Here lies the body
Of Harriet Hick,
Stuffed with chocolate.
Sick! Sick! Sick!

Here lies the body
Of Patrick Jones:
Ate a whole elephant,
Skin and bones!

By John Kitching

Now you try it

1 Copy out these sentences. Choose a word or two from the Belinda Brewer and Henry Hurst poems to fill the gaps.

Example:

Belinda went for a...

Belinda went for a *swim*.

a Belinda swam in the...

b Here lies the body of H...

c Henry was so full of food his...

What do we know about the characters?

1   Choose one of the characters and make up a play about that person.

Example

Percy Peat

Henry: *(holding his nose)* Phew, Percy. You stink!

Wendy: *(chewing a pie)* It's your feet. Don't take off your shoes.

Percy: Well, you can talk. You're eating a mince pie and it's full of flies.

Wendy: *(munches pie)* It tastes good!

Percy: My feet don't stink!

Henry: They stink so much, you'll die smelling them.

Percy: Ha, ha. *(Smells feet)* Oh, uggggh!

From reading the poem, you know that Percy's feet smell and he dies. You have some information about Percy before you write the play.

2   In groups, act out your short play. See what the rest of the class think about the play.

3   Now write a sentence or two about Harriet Hick.

You know she loves chocolate and can't stop eating it.

You will also need to make up some facts.

- What does she look like?
- Where does she live?
- Does she have any brothers or sisters?
- What are her hobbies?

Level Booster

LEVEL 2

- I can read out parts of a performance poem
- I can understand a performance poem
- I can understand events in short poems

LEVEL 3

- I can read performance poems with some expression
- I can write my own performance poem
- I can understand characters' feelings

LEVEL 4

- I can understand the way a character is thinking and feeling
- I can read performance poetry with expression
- I can understand how characters' feelings change as I read on

Chapter 4

AF4 Identify and comment on the structure and organisation of texts, including grammatical and presentational features at text level

This chapter is going to show you how to

- Understand what makes an exciting start to a story
- Understand what makes an amazing middle
- Understand what makes an exciting end.

What's it all about?

You will be able to recognise good starts, middles and endings to stories.

Getting you thinking

Read the story and decide why you think it is or is not a good start to a story.

The Mighty Skink *by Paul Shipton*

I remember the day Skink arrived like it only just happened. I remember it so well 'cos it was the day that things changed forever.

I spent the morning just swinging around the outer branches of the Big Tree. It was my most favourite spot in the whole wide world. Every once in a while I let out this great big whoop, like this:

'WHOOOOOOOOOO – UP!
WHOOOOOOOOOO – UP!'

It's not easy to get a whoop just right, you know. You've got to start it right deep down in your belly, then kind of build it up in your chest, so it gets louder and louder, until it rises at the end for the final -UP! bit.

Don't go thinking I was up there just to practise my whooping noises though. I wanted

to get some good thinking done, and you couldn't do *that* down on the ground with the rest of the Tribe all chattering around you and making a din. That's why the Big Tree was really good – you could scoot up it and almost feel like you were on your own. But the best bit was, it had this great view of what was outside our Enclosure. What I'd do, I'd climb up to my branch and spend hours just looking out across The Fence.

Chim, who was my best friend – even though I'd never tell him that in a million years – he always said that I spent too much time thinking. He said that I'd wear my brain out with thinking too much, and I'd end up this crazy old monkey that couldn't even unzip a banana for myself. Hah!

How does it work?

The extract is the start of an exciting story. The writer wants the story to be as exciting as possible, so you can't put the book down.

Now you try it

Plan a story about spiders by jotting down at least four or five good ideas. Think of an amazing title for your story.

If you cannot think of a good title you could use 'Spider Attack'.

If you are stuck for ideas, you could include the following ideas:

- Spiders are in a lab.
- Scientists have experimented on the spiders.
- The spiders have become intelligent.
- The spiders want to take over the world.

Development activity APP

The Amazing Start – Book Prize

1 Imagine 'The Mighty Skink' has won a prize for an amazing start to a book. You are writing a speech for the award ceremony. In your speech you should mention the book's **good** points.

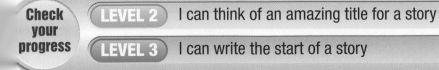

Getting you thinking

If the middle of a story is boring, readers might lose interest. Look at the two examples – which is best and why?

Amelia's Nightmare

1 Amelia sat in the café. She sipped her coffee and wondered what had happened to her dad. She'd spent ages trying to find him. She'd got nowhere.

The waiter came up to her and told her to go. He needed to close the café. She wanted to text her friends, to tell them she was safe. She looked down at her mobile. The battery was low.

She didn't like the look in the waiter's eyes. She knew she had to leave. She picked up her rucksack and walked towards the door. Outside, it was raining. This was going to be a long night.

'I know a place you can stay,' said the waiter.

Amelia shivered. He'd read her thoughts.

2 Amelia sat in the café. She was tired and her head ached. She must find her dad. She needed to find clues from somewhere.

The waiter smiled at her, shrugging his shoulders. 'Time to go, love. I'm shutting up in a few moments,' he said.

He smiled, but there was something about him she didn't like. She distrusted him. His eyes were watery blue, his smile too friendly. She shivered.

She glanced at her mobile, gripped in her cold hands. The battery was low. She couldn't text her friends. She couldn't let them know where she was or how she was feeling.

Amelia stood up from the table. She adjusted her rucksack and walked towards the battered café door. By now the rain was hammering on the roof. This was going to be a long night.

'I know a place you can stay,' hissed the waiter.

Amelia shivered. He'd read her thoughts.

How does it work?

One story is more exciting than the other.

The first one tells us the same story but the second makes the story more exciting. It does this by giving us more detail.

- We now know Amelia was tired and her head ached.

- We also discover more about the waiter – the way he looks and speaks. Amelia does not trust him.

- We also learn more about the café. The door is damaged. It has seen better days!

Now you try it

1 If there is space, walk around the room as if you are the waiter. Is he meant to be good or bad? How would he walk? How would he look?

2 Read the sentences you have written for the start of your story about spiders.

Can you make them more interesting?

Can you describe your characters in more detail?

Can you write more about what is happening?

3 Continue your story by making an exciting middle.

Development activity APP

Towards an awesome end

What could happen next in the story to make it exciting?

Below are some ideas.

- Amelia is taken to some old buildings. The waiter tries to keep her a prisoner. She sends one text to a friend before the battery dies.

- Her friend from school, Joel Harman, rescues her. The police capture the waiter.

- Amelia's dad works for the bank. He has gone into hiding to escape the gang. They were trying to force him to rob the bank.

- Amelia finds out that her dad is at her great aunt's house. He'd once killed someone in a hit and run accident. He'd kept the accident a secret. The gang were blackmailing him.

Stories are best when planned. The writer has thought of four or five ideas to keep the story interesting. They will lead on to an awesome end.

Can you think of any better ideas?

Check your progress

| LEVEL 2 | I can recognise a good and bad story |
| LEVEL 3 | I can describe characters using some detail |

Getting you thinking

The ending of a story is important. The end leaves the reader with a good or poor impression of the book.

Here are some ideas for the end of 'Amelia's Nightmare'.

The End

- The police surround a hut. The gang are inside the hut. They are not giving up without a fight.

- Amelia can see that her dad is in the hut, captured by the gang.

- The gang were using Amelia's dad as a hostage. However, Joel Harman is also in the hut, hiding. He springs at the gang leader. The gangster's gun spins from his hand. The police charge the hut. For Amelia, it's all a blur. Dad is rescued and Joel is a hero.

How does it work?

The ending is exciting; it keeps you interested until the final moment. The ending is complete as the gang are captured. There's no chance of getting bored … is there?

Now you try it APP

See if you can come up with an exciting end for your story.

Use bullet points for three to five ideas that could happen in your story about the spiders. The ideas should help you write an awesome end.

Write four or five sentences to complete your story.

Development activity

Read your stories to each other and perform the best one.

Check your progress

| LEVEL 2 | I can write a story |
| LEVEL 3 | I can write a planned story |

Level Booster

- I can recognise a start to a story
- I can recognise an ending of a story
- I can write the start of a story

- I can recognise a good start to a story
- I can recognise how a writer keeps a story interesting
- I can recognise a good ending

- I can recognise how the story is linked together
- I can recognise how a story is shaped
- I can link ideas in my own story

Chapter 5

AF5 Explain and comment on writers' use of language, including grammatical and literary features at word and sentence level

This chapter is going to show you how to

- Recognise word choices in a traditional tale
- Recognise word choices in a modern tale.

What's it all about?

Stories change as they are retold by different tellers to different listeners. You already know a lot about what usually happens in fairy stories and folk tales.

Getting you thinking

What language choices are used when writing traditional fairy tales? Your teacher will read a traditional fairy tale to you.

The Princess and the Frog

Once upon a time there lived a king. He had a beautiful daughter. They lived in a big castle. Near the castle there was a dark forest. In the forest, under an old lime-tree, was a deep well. The king's daughter went near the well when she was bored. She took a ball with her and she played throw and catch. She played throw and catch on her own.

One day the ball fell into the well. The ball sank in the water. The king's daughter was so sad that she cried. Then something spoke from the well.

'What's the matter, king's daughter? Why are you crying?'

When the princess looked around, all she could see was a frog. Its big, ugly head popped from the water.

'I'm crying because my ball has fallen into the well,' sobbed the princess.

The frog croaked.

'What will you give me if I find your ball at the bottom of the well?'

The princess thought for a moment.

'You can have anything I own. <u>Pearls</u>, <u>jewels</u>, even my <u>golden crown</u>.'

The frog thought for a moment and answered, 'I don't care for your <u>pearls</u>, <u>jewels</u> or your <u>golden crown</u>. I just want to be your friend.'

The princess agreed and the frog found her ball. The princess grabbed the ball and ran off. She did not trust a talking frog and she did not want to be friends with something so ugly. She ran all the way to the king, who was counting money in the palace counting room.

The princess told her father everything. The king told her that she had to keep her promise. She hated the ugly cold frog and she did not want to see the frog again. The king grew angry.

'The frog helped you when you were in trouble. You must not hate him now.'

The princess found the frog and carried it to her room. She wanted to lie down and rest. The frog looked at her with his big <u>bulging</u> eyes.

'Let me lie next to you,' he <u>croaked</u>.
'I'm tired too.'

The princess grew angry. She picked the frog up and threw him against the wall.

'Now be quiet, you horrible little frog,' she cried.

When she looked down, the frog had turned into a handsome prince.

'I was <u>bewitched</u> and turned into a frog by a wicked witch. I had to remain a frog until a princess took me into her room.'

The prince and princess married and lived happily ever after.

How does it work?

Have you noticed how traditional fairy tales usually start with 'Once upon a time' and end with 'lived happily ever after'?

Now you try it

1   Working in pairs, see how many typical things and characters from fairy stories you can note down.

2   Write down as many titles of folk and fairy stories as you can think of.

Here are a few to get you started:

Typical things	Titles	Characters
Frogs	Cinderella	
Forests	Rumplestiltskin	

3   Look in the library or on the internet and see if you can find some traditional tales. See how they start and end.

Development activity APP

The writer's choice of words

The author chooses some interesting words. These have been underlined in the story for you.

The author could have written 'he said' but used the word 'croaked', to make the frog sound like a frog. Using the word 'bulging' gives us the idea the frog's eyes were almost popping out of his head.

The reason the author uses words such as 'pearls', 'jewels' and 'golden crown' is because he wants to make the princess sound rich.

Look at the traditional tale you have chosen and see if you can find some words the author has used to make the tale more interesting.

Check your progress

LEVEL 2   I can recognise a traditional tale

LEVEL 3   I can recognise a writer's word choices

Notice how the writer makes different word choices for a modern version of the same story.

The Princess and the Frog
(A modern version)

In the old days there lived a king. He had a daughter who was a spoiled brat. They lived in a big castle and she had everything she needed – except a friend. She'd fallen out with all her friends.

She used to play with a big ball near a well in the forest. She did this because she was bored and lonely and had no friends.

One day the ball fell into the well and floated away. Because she was spoiled, the princess began to cry. She only stopped crying when she heard somebody asking her what was wrong.

When the princess wiped her eyes, she noticed a big ugly frog with bulging eyes.

It was in the water.

'I'm crying because my ball has floated to the middle of the well. Now I'm speaking to a talking frog. I must be going mad!'

The princess sobbed even more. She offered the frog all she owned, including her pearls, jewels and golden crown. The stupid, ugly frog didn't want anything of value; he just wanted to go wherever she went. The princess readily agreed. She knew she could outrun a frog!

'Yeah, whatever!' she said.

'Cool,' croaked the frog and he swam to the ball.

The princess grabbed the ball and ran.

'Wait for me,' said the frog.

The princess gave a cruel laugh.

'No way! I don't trust a talking frog. I'm not being a friend with anything so ugly. It'd ruin my image. And don't think I'm going to kiss you. Uggggg!'

The princess ran back to the castle and told her dad everything. He was angry. He told his daughter that the frog had helped her when she was in trouble, so she should help the frog now. The princess turned pale.

'Dream on, dad. I'm not being a friend with a horrid, ugly frog.'

The king was angry. He told his daughter she'd do as she was told or he'd banish her from the country. She'd have nowhere to go. She'd become poor. She'd have to work for a living! The princess quickly found the frog and took it to her room. She lay on her bed and threw the frog against the castle wall.

'Now be quiet forever, you horrid lump of hopping jelly,' she cried. 'Hope I've killed you!'

A prince stood up. 'Well, you've given me a few bruises,' he said.

The princess eyed the prince up and down. He wasn't bad looking. He'd do! They married in haste and the prince soon regretted marrying the spoiled princess. She nagged him to an early death.

How does it work?

The author uses some words to give the tale a modern feel. Examples: 'Cool' and 'whatever'. Have you noticed that the traditional start and ending have changed? This makes the tale sound modern.

Now you try it

Pick out other words that the author has chosen to make it seem modern.

Development activity APP

1 Re-writing stories is nothing new. Fairy stories and folk tales were meant to be entertaining, but they also had other uses.

Fairy stories often give a warning to children. The most common dangers children face in fairy stories are listed below. Make a list of stories you know in which these different dangers can be found.

Stories I remember...	Children in danger from...
	Giants and ogres
	Witches
	Evil spirits

2 Choose a fairy story or folk tale you know yourself and write the first part of it, as if it were a modern story.

Start by making a plan like the one below:

Traditional story: Snow White	My modern version: Ebony Black
Beginning: *Once upon a time in a faraway kingdom…*	**Beginning:** *It happened one time in a country far away…*
Main events: 1 *There is a princess called Snow White.* 2 *She has a jealous stepmother who has a magic mirror.*	Main events: 1 *There is a princess called Ebony Black.* 2 *She has a jealous stepmother who has a magic computer.*

Level Booster

LEVEL 2

- I can recognise some language choices
- I know why some stories use traditional language
- I know why writers choose some words

LEVEL 3

- I can recognise why writers make certain choices
- I can pick out some words writers use for effect
- I can make simple comments about writers' language choices

LEVEL 4

- I can recognise and explain why writers make language choices
- I can comment on certain word choices
- I can rewrite stories using different choices of words

Chapter 6

AF6 Identify and comment on writers' purposes and viewpoints, and the overall effect of the text on the reader

This chapter is going to show you how to

- Recognise a viewpoint
- Recognise different opinions.

What's it all about?

Noticing that writers have viewpoints.

Getting you thinking

Everyone has opinions about things.
Some people may want to disagree with other people's opinions because they have their own.

Nathan: I think Manchester United is the best football club in Britain.

Joanne: No way. Liverpool is the best. They've won the league title more times than any other club.

Devdatta: It's good to take exercise, stay fit and eat healthy food.

Wayne: Exercise is boring. I like eating burgers; they're tastier than healthy stuff. It's great being on the computer or watching films.

Clara: I love English. The lessons are so interesting.

Leroi: What a joke! All we do is read or write. Maths is far more fun.

How does it work?

We are all different and think differently about things. We have viewpoints that others may disagree with.

Now you try it

In groups, which viewpoints do you agree with? Why?

Development activity APP

List five viewpoints that somebody might have. Then list five different viewpoints.

Example:

Viewpoint: Liverpool is the best team in the Premier League.

Different viewpoint: Arsenal is the best team in the Premier League.

Check your progress

| LEVEL 2 | I can recognise a viewpoint |
| LEVEL 3 | I can recognise various viewpoints |

Getting you thinking

Read the letter and work out what opinions the writer has expressed.

Dear Head teacher,

All children are horrible, but your students are worse than any I have ever seen. They are a disgrace!

Your students wear their uniform but it looks a mess. Their ties are undone and their shoes need a good clean. The boys' trousers are muddy and their shirts are torn.

In my view, you should line them all up in the playground and check the state of their uniforms. If the uniforms are scruffy they should all be sent home.

I demand you reply to this letter.

Yours sincerely,

Desmond Worldwise

Now you try it

Write a letter the head teacher might send to Desmond Worldwise, replying to his letter.

Development activity **APP**

Dear Head teacher,

I'm a Year 9 student. The sport offered in our school is not really for everyone – most people hate it.

I wrote out a survey and asked Year 7, 8 and 9 kids what they'd like to do to keep healthy. Street dancing came out tops!

Some younger teachers were interested and I've booked the use of the gym after school. We dance for an hour, twice a week.

The whole thing has really taken off. Some sixth-formers run the street dancing sessions and about fifty people of all ages come along.

We all feel fitter and healthier!

Sonya Harper

1   In groups, think about something that you could do to be healthier.

Check your progress

LEVEL 2 I can write a simple letter

LEVEL 3 I can write a letter expressing a viewpoint

Level Booster

LEVEL 2

- I can recognise a viewpoint
- I can express my opinions
- I can think of five different viewpoints

LEVEL 3

- I can understand different viewpoints
- I can comment on a writers' viewpoint
- I can reply to a letter, giving a different viewpoint

LEVEL 4

- I can write about my opinions
- I can explain about different viewpoints
- I can clearly express my opinions on different subjects

Chapter 7

AF7 Relate texts to their social, cultural and historical traditions

This chapter is going to show you how to

- Recognise stories from the past, the future and from other places
- Recognise local stories.

What's it all about?

Knowing where and when stories are set.

Look at the story extracts. Can you guess which story is set now or in the future, which is set in the past and which is from a different place?

1   In Ancient Time

Like the wind through the trees before the rain, we always knew when the story was coming. He would wait for a silence around the fire, lean forward warming his hands, and begin.

'In ancient time before any of you were even born, I was a young man. No cursed Roman soldier had yet set foot in this land of ours. We were not then a beaten people. We were wild perhaps, quarrelsome certainly, but we were our own people.'

2   Transvaal

Once, during the Malaria season in the Eastern Transvaal, it seemed to me, when I was in high fever and like to die, that the whole world was a big burial ground.

3   The Planet Minor X1

We had landed. The ground seemed hostile. I could see tiny creatures move amongst the blue tufts of grass. Some of these creatures could be dangerous, especially if they had taken guns from the stockade.

I aimed my own gun and fired. I shot the creature and it melted, not leaving a trace of its icy existence.

How does it work?

Each title and each story gives us a few clues as to when or where it was set. Can you spot the clues?

Now you try it

In groups, work out which story is set now or in the future, which is set in the past and which is from a different place.

Development activity APP

In pairs, write a few sentences describing a setting from the past, present or future. See if your partner can recognise where and when the story is set.

Check your progress

| LEVEL 2 | I can recognise where a story is set |
| LEVEL 3 | I can write a simple story set in the present, past or future |

Getting you thinking

Do you know any stories from your area?

In small groups, try to think of any story you might know. It could be a smuggling story or a ghost story. Something amazing might have happened to someone you know.

Here is a story from the Isle of Man.

The Black Dog

A grumpy old man used to live in a place called Peel. The old man was called Juan Cortlett. He was a smuggler and he owned a big black dog. It was bigger than most dogs and it was very vicious.

One night he was out with his dog and he was waiting for a ship. Inside the ship was some fine French lace. It sold well on the black market in England. He had made a deal with the French Captain. If he sold the lace he'd become rich!

The coastguards knew about the smugglers and they were waiting for Old Juan Cortlett. They shot him and his dog. Both were killed instantly.

Now, on a dark windy night, you can still hear Cortlett's dog and some say they have seen the dog. It looks as big as a horse and it barks like twenty dogs.

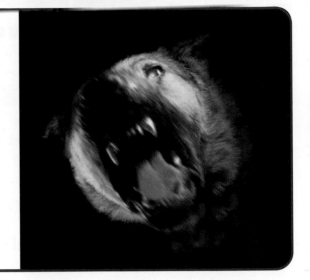

How does it work?

When people write a story from an area, they need to find out information about the area.

Now you try it

Gather as much information as you can about a story from the area you live in. Bullet point about six or seven ideas.

Development activity

Retell to the class a story from the area you live in.

Check your progress

| LEVEL 2 | I can recognise stories from other countries |
| LEVEL 3 | I can retell a story from my area |

Level Booster

LEVEL 2

- I know books are set in different times and places
- I know some books are set in other countries
- I know books can be set on other planets

LEVEL 3

- I can recognise books with historical settings
- I can recognise books set in other countries
- I can tell stories known in my area

LEVEL 4

- I can see why some books are set in different times and places
- I can describe a setting from the past, present or future
- I can tell and write about a story from my local area

Teacher Guide

Where the final task of the double-page section is substantial enough to provide a snapshot of students' progress, this has been marked as an **APP opportunity**.

Each double-page section ends with a **Check your progress** box. This offers a levelled checklist against which students can self- or peer-assess their final piece of writing from the **Development** or **Now you try it** section.

The end of chapter **Level Booster** is a less task-specific checklist of the skills students need to master to reach Level 2, 3 and 4. It can be used to help students see the level they are working at currently and to visualise what they need to do to make progress.

This book acknowledges the fact that students aiming for Level 3 will perform better if they are given starter activities that relate to the work they need to learn. The activities will appeal to students with different learning styles

Chapter 1 AF1 Use a range of strategies, including accurate decoding of text, to read for meaning

STARTER 1

Read the story on page 6, 'The Cool Gang', to pupils. Read the story again, this time slowly and with emphasis. Instruct pupils to raise a hand each time they hear a word they do not understand. To reinforce unknown words, instruct students to say a sentence using these words.

For example: People wear **jackets** to keep warm. Gangs wear **hoods** over their heads.

Now ask the students to read the story. Students could take turns and read a sentence each. If any student stumbles over a word, ask students to say a sentence using the word causing difficulty.

For example: She **wore** a new coat. He could see their **faces** through the window.

STARTER 2

I spy

If students struggle with the alphabet, here are some suggestions to help with their learning.

As a lesson starter, play the traditional I spy game:

Say, 'I spy with my little eye, something beginning with…' and add the initial letter.

Play the game, but if students do not realise what the 'B' in the room is, let your eyes wander to the object – say, 'book'. Should students still not guess the object, point to the book. It might be possible for students to try the 'I Spy' game in small groups.

One way of learning the alphabet is to chant it in groups. Or give students printed copies of the alphabet, to say aloud, chant and learn.

1 Understand stories

Getting you thinking

Model the story by reading it to students.

How does it work?

Once students have read a sentence of the story, some may want to read a paragraph or more. Encourage students to follow your reading and the reading of others in their books.

Now you try it

Allow students to read more than a few sentences. The emphasis is on reading to others. Encourage students to read with expression.

Development

You may want to photocopy this exercise rather than asking students to copy the sentences into their books. However, the answers should be written in full sentences. Reinforce starting every sentence with a capital letter and ending with a full stop.

Extension activity

Check to see if students have understood the story by getting them to answer the following questions:

1 Why do you think the gang all wore hoods?

2 Why do you think the gang all wore the same jackets?

3 Do you think the gang members were soft or tough?

2 Understand a problem page

Getting you thinking

Students should read the problem pages in small groups. However, model the reading to them first.

How does it work?

Readers should not spend all their time looking at the script. Instruct students to keep eye contact with members of the group. This helps the group to focus on the reader.

Students should be encouraged to speak loud enough to be heard by all, if reading to the class, or to be audible to their group but not everyone else in the room, if they are reading in groups. Remind the reader to read aloud but not to shout!

Students should be made aware of pace. If they speak too slowly, the groups' attention may wander. If they speak too fast, the group may not be able to follow the storyline and will not be able to understand what is being read.

Some students may need practice with this.

Now you try it

Some possible additions to Misha's advice might be:

The Ex-friend
- Speak to the ex-friend calmly about the problem; see if you can be friends again.
- Speak to your parent(s) about the problem.
- See your head of year.

Ask students, in groups, to reply to the other two letters Misha received. Possible advice might include:

The Bullied
- Stay with a group of friends so you can't be singled out.
- Speak to your parent(s) about the problem.
- Contact the police: you have the evidence if pictures go on the internet.

The Boyfriend
- Have a word with Mum. See if she can spend some time with you. Show her it isn't fair as she used to spend lots of time with you and now you feel rejected.
- Ask your brother how he manages to get on with Mum's new boyfriend.
- Try and find out what interests the new boyfriend and join in.

78

Development

Read this letter to your students.

> Dear Misha,
>
> I am worried. I enjoy the excitement of stealing things. I steal from sweetshops and from my friends' sports bags.
>
> This morning, I nicked £20 from my mum's purse. I'm worried I'll get caught.
>
> What should I do?
>
> Stephen.

Tell your students to write a reply to Stephen. Is Stephen worried because he'll get caught or worried because he steals? What do you think?

When replying, students should point out that it is wrong to steal. If Stephen steals from his own mother, he is breaking her trust. If Stephen steals, he will get caught sooner or later. The consequences will be severe. Students may also suggest that Stephen needs help from others.

3 Read and understand a poem

Getting you thinking

Read the poem to the group, so that they are able to understand it.

How does it work?

Ask students what they find funny about the poem. Ask them where they think the emphasis should go when they read aloud – and why.

Now you try it

Ask students to read the poem aloud, with expression. Ask them to place the emphasis in the places you did.

Development

If students cannot work out what is embarrassing in the first verse, point it out. You may want to photocopy the written answers section.

Allow students to work in groups on these exercises.

> ## Chapter 2 AF2 Understand, describe, select or retrieve information, events or ideas from texts and use quotation and reference to text

STARTER 1

Personal Space

If you have access to a school hall or a drama room, students can think of different ways of moving through their personal space.

These movements should include

- walking
- walking with a limp
- crawling
- rolling
- hopping
- skipping
- jumping
- leaping
- walking on tiptoes
- walking backwards.

Allow students to do this activity for about ten minutes.

When the activity is over, encourage them to think about different ways of walking.

- Allow students to **walk** around the space as they wish. Some may march, others stride, and others may walk slowly.
- Then ask them to walk as **slowly** as they can. Then ask them to walk, with care, as quickly as they can. They can then walk with a **limp**.
- Then ask them to walk as **high** as they can – on tiptoes.
- They can then walk as **low** as they can – by slouching.
- They can walk as **lightly** as they can – like a ballet dancer, or as **heavily** as they can – like a footballer who's just scored an own goal or been sent off.

- Students can then walk **directly** – from point to point. Or they can walk **indirectly** – wandering aimlessly, say with hands in pockets.

- They can walk changing the **focus** of the movement, meaning they can alter their facial expressions and gaze. Usually, this automatically changes their body curve.

- They can then think of an unhappy person – walking aimlessly, perhaps staring at the floor. Or a businessman in a hurry, eyes fixed forward. Or a happy person, who might stride out, chin up.

In this Starter, choose students who do particularly well with the activity and allow them to model their work to the rest of the group.

Explain to students that they have 'been' different characters. Our facial expressions, body language and the way we move show others our personality and our mood. Allow one student to model being happy. As the group watch, ask them the following questions:

- How do we know the character is happy? Is the character (or student name) walking high or low? Is the student walking fast or slow? Is the student looking ahead or glaring at the floor? Is the student walking heavy or light?

Students should then recognise what a happy or sad person would be like.

Ask individual students to model other emotions – such as anger, being upset, frightened or excited.

Tell them they are going to look at and write about different characters. When they write about characters, they need to think about how the characters would walk, talk, think and behave – depending upon their moods.

1 Look at characters in non-fiction

Getting you thinking

Explain to students the differences between fiction and non-fiction. If possible, take them to the library and ask them to find a fiction and a non-fiction book.

Model the extract by reading it to the students.

How does it work?

Show students a map of Australia. Point out Melbourne in the south and show them how far Robert Burke and the team had to trek to reach the north coast.

Now you try it

You may wish to photocopy these questions.

Otherwise, students should copy the questions into their books and leave gaps for the answers. Try to persuade students to write the answers using full sentences.

Development

If students cannot work out Robert Burke's mistakes, point them out.

Explain to students what 'hot seating' is.

2 Make decisions about characters

Getting you thinking

Explain that characters have good and bad points. Allow students to discover the merits and demerits of these four teenagers from the descriptions. Allow the students to make their own judgements about why they would or would not befriend a character.

Ask students to be one of the four characters and 'hot seat' that character. By keeping in role students have to defend their characters, thinking about their way of life and how they behave.

Students can then write an event in the life of their character.

Example: Jason Smart

- Jason takes a ten-pound note from the maths teacher's pocket.

- The maths teacher realises his money has gone. He is upset, as the ten-pound note was to buy his daughter a birthday present.

- The class is sympathetic but they don't know who has taken the money.

- It's break time and the class file out of the classroom.

- Jim Fullerton, a member of Jason's form, knows Jason is a pickpocket. He confronts Jason, who denies taking any money. He claims he has no money with him.

- At the dining hall, Jason is spotted buying lots of food and drink. He is about to hand the money over to the dinner lady. Jim and the rest of his form surround him. Students tell him he is mean and wrong and they'll tell the maths teacher he has stolen the money.
- Jason pleads with his peers and they agree to a plan.
- Jason finds the maths teacher, and tells him he went back to the maths room and searched for the money. He discovered the £10 note stuffed behind a radiator.

3 Characters in fiction

Getting you thinking

Model the story by reading it to students. If necessary, explain more challenging vocabulary such as 'flair' and 'hoist'. You might also like to tell students that Catherine of Alexandria lived in the fourth century. Ask students what they think of Damian.

How does it work?

Tell the students that the scene is taking place in a classroom and that Mr Quinn is the teacher. Explain that Damian is different from the other students in the classroom. He fails to understand that he should stop talking. Explain that although the teacher is polite to Damian, he is aware that the class have started to talk amongst themselves.

- The maths teacher is thankful and praises Jason!

When students write or bullet point their story, they must keep the character in role.

Now you try it

Allow pupils to write their own profiles in any format they wish. They can type them on a word processor, using their ICT skills.

Now you try it

Give students some prompts about what to look out for: Mr Gum's likes, dislikes, appearance, behaviour, for instance.

Students should have noted
- Mr Gum hates children, animals, fun and cartoons.
- He stays in bed all day. He is lazy.
- He enjoys being evil.
- He draws scowls on his forehead – which is unusual!
- He sticks things in his beard.

Development

Students should add things about their own character, which is not a reworking of their profile.

> ## Chapter 3 AF3 Deduce, infer or interpret information, events or ideas from texts

STARTER 1

What would you do?

Students take on the role of a character. The character can be invented or can be a famous person known to all. You ask the student 'What would the character do if…?'

- The character saw a derelict building and walked into it, and noticed somebody slumped on a chair. (Student can mime walking into the building and mime what they would do.)
- The person slumped on the chair has their face cast downwards, so you can't see who it is.

What would you do? (Again, the student can mime the action.)

- Whatever you thought you would do, you actually go up to the person and lift up their face. Then you get a shock – you are looking at yourself! (The student can mime the action.)

It is a good idea to get all the students working on this at the same time. The aim of the exercise is to allow students to work out how a character might feel in a particular situation. It should put them in others' shoes **before** they write anything.

Do you have a brother or sister?

Before students are introduced to the poems, ask them if they have a brother or sister. (If not, a cousin, uncle or aunt?)

In pairs, **A** can talk about their brother or sister. **B** listens.

- Is the brother or sister older or younger?
- What does the brother/sister like or dislike?

- What is the brother/sister good at, not so good at?
- Does A clash with his/her brother or sister? Or are they the best of friends?

Students then swap roles.

In groups, all the Bs should try to remember what they discovered about A's brother/sister. Then roles are swapped and the As must remember all they can about B's brother or sister.

1 Understand characters' feelings

Getting you thinking

Ask students how they get on with their brother(s) and/or sister(s). Allow a free discussion.

Then read the poem to the students.

How does it work?

Ask students to think of things they really like/dislike about a brother or sister.

Now you try it

Ask students to pick out three things they think the sister would find most annoying.

Development

Allow students to work on the questions on their own or in pairs. Students may need some help with the more challenging vocabulary, such as 'excrutiating', 'smarminess' and 'over-rated'.

2 Understand feelings through performance poetry

Getting you thinking

Model the poem for the students by reading it to them, using **two** voices.

How does it work?

Explain to the students how you can tell the teacher's voice from Blenkinsop's voice.

Discuss how the poet makes the poem funny by listing all Blenkinsop's ridiculous excuses.

Now you try it

Students should be allowed a few tries at the poem until they are happy with their performance.

Development

If students are unsure of the task, they could use the writing frame below.

Late again…
Your tea is…
What's your excuse…?
Sorry mum. It's…

Whose fault…?

It's my P.E. teacher, …

Why is it his fault, Adrian?

He kept me…

Why did he…?

Because I told… grandma, mum.

Yes, but grandma is still…

I know, but I…

3 Understand short poems

Getting you thinking

You may want to explain that 'R.I.P.' stands for 'rest in peace'. Students could read the poems in small groups.

How does it work?

Allow students to talk about the poems, pointing out what is happening in each one.

Now you try it

Students should work in pairs during this exercise.

Development

Students might need to be reminded of how to set out a play.

Chapter 4 AF4 Identify and comment on the structure and organisation of texts, including grammatical and presentational features at text level

1 Understand what makes an exciting start to a story

Getting you thinking

You might want to explain what is happening in the story.

- The story is told to us by a monkey – later on in the story we find out his name is Giz.

- Giz is talking about a new arrival named Skink.

- Giz mentions how to 'whoop' and he tells us how it is done.

- Giz has a favourite tree; it's called the big tree. We discover that Giz does not like spending time with the other monkeys. He likes being alone, thinking.

- We then discover that Giz is not free: he is in an enclosure. He is fenced in. This comes as a bit of a shock.

- Giz has a friend, called Chim. Chim believes Giz is spending too much time thinking. Chim believes that thinking is dangerous. He warns Giz that if he spends too much time thinking, he'll end up wearing his brains out!

Ask the students what they think might happen next. Students could get into groups and work out what sort of a character Skink might be. Why will he be mighty?

Ask students what they think will happen next.

How does it work?

Ask students if they liked the story. Did they think it was exciting? Can they think of a story they know which is more exciting?

Development

Instead of talking about 'The Mighty Skink', students could talk about books they like and they think start in an exciting way. Students should mention some good points about the start of their chosen book.

2 Understand what makes an amazing middle

Getting you thinking

Explain to students the story so far: Amelia has bunked off school. She arrives home and is in her bedroom when her dad arrives. She sneaks a look downstairs. In the hallway are her dad and two strangers. They argue and threaten her dad. One hits him on the nose. Later, her dad vanishes. Amelia goes in search of him.

Then model the story by reading it to the students.

How does it work?

Allow students to spot the difference between the two extracts.

Now you try it

The students could act out the story so far. This will make the characters clearer in their minds, as they will be able to envisage the body language.

Students could read out their spider stories and then redraft them.

Development

To help them understand the development and end of the story 'Amelia's Nightmare', students could draw a storyboard of the events. Students can either bullet point their own stories or storyboard their ideas before they write the middle of their stories.

3 Understand what makes an exciting end

Getting you thinking

Students could act out their own alternative scenarios.

How does it work?

Question students and discuss whether they feel the ending was good. Check that they understood the story.

Now you try it

Check that students are planning their story. They can use bullet points, a flowchart or a storyboard.

Development

Encourage students to read their finished stories to each other.

Chapter 5 AF5 Explain and comment on writers' use of language, including grammatical and literary features at word and sentence level

STARTER 1

Once upon a time

These activities are based on the belief that children know a great deal about stories, their structure and their conventions. The activities are based on the premise that literature is something to be thought about and talked about, not just consumed. They aim to develop students' understanding of texts and the societies which produced them and in which they are read.

Mention to students that many traditional stories begin with 'Once upon a time…'.

Allow students to sit in a circle. Start the game by saying 'Once upon a time… there lived a wicked witch.'

Tell students they have to say what happened next.

Example:

You: Once upon a time there lived a wicked witch.

Student 1: She liked to eat people.

Student 2: First she captured a young boy.

Student 3: Next she put him in a cooking pot.

Student 4: But he managed to escape.

You might want to complete the story.

You: The witch fell into her own pot and was boiled!

STARTER 2

You could then try a modern story.

You: Once upon a time – a gang roamed the streets.

The starter exercises should give students a sense of story structure.

Ask students what fairy stories they know. Remind them of 'Little Red Riding Hood' or 'Goldilocks and the Three Bears' or 'Jack and the Beanstalk'.

Tell them that these stories have been around for centuries. They were told even before they were written down. Many of the stories are known throughout the world in different versions.

In groups, ask them to tell each other a fairy tale. See how many fairy tales they know.

When students tell their stories, remind them about eye contact, tone of voice, pace, volume and body language. You may want them to have the following information:

- **Eye contact** – Look at other people in your group now and again. It helps to keep their attention.
- **Tone of voice** – Vary your tone of voice, this will stop people in the group becoming bored.
- **Pace** – avoid speaking too slowly or too fast.
- **Volume** – Try to speak loud enough to be heard, without shouting. Raise your voice at certain times when you are speaking the words your character has said.
- **Body Language** – Look confident. Use a few hand gestures.

1 Recognise word choices in a traditional tale

Getting you thinking

Model 'The Princess and the Frog' story by reading it to students.

How does it work?

Students may have spotted the fairytale conventions, but if not, point them out in the story.

Now you try it

Most school libraries will have a book of traditional fairy tales, if not there are plenty of examples on the internet. For example: http://www.bbc.co.uk/cbeebies/stories/redriding hood.shtml

Development

Show students the underlined words and explain why the author has chosen to use them.

2 Recognise word choices in a modern tale

Getting you thinking

Model the story to the students by reading it to them. Explain to students that as you read the story you want them to notice how the language differs from the first extract. Ask them what makes it a modern story.

How does it work?

Students may have noticed the difference between the two stories. However, if they have failed to do so, point it out to them.

Now you try it

Allow students to pick out the modern words. They could make a chart.

Development

Encourage pupils to explore the messages of folk and fairy tales written in different places at different times.

1 Students can choose a tale they have already found in the library or on the internet.

2 Once students have turned part of the traditional tale into a modern one, they can read it to the rest of the group.

STARTER 1

Allow students to sit in a circle. Ask them to say something that is true.

Examples:

Our uniform is blue.

The sun warms planet Earth.

I have a pet dog.

Our desks are made of wood.

Now ask students to say something that is a point of view.

- Andy Murray is the best tennis player in Britain.
- My mum's the best mum in the world.
- Science lessons are a waste of time.
- Motorbikes are better than cars.
- The world will end in twenty year's time.

Point out that viewpoints are a matter of opinion. They might be true but often are not!

Allow students to look at the following statements. In small groups, they should decide which statements are true and which are not.

1 Being at school is a waste of time.

2 My dog is the most vicious dog in town.

3 On Saturday we don't go to school.

4 Cod is a type of fish.

5 Apples come from trees.

6 Cabbage tastes awful.

Allow students to send an envoy to another group. Have both groups got the same answers? Ask students to discuss and see if they can come up with a common agreement.

STARTER 2

In pairs, students should have viewpoints about their likes and dislikes.

A gives his viewpoints and **B** agrees or disagrees. After five minutes, they swap roles.

Example:

A: I don't like getting up in the mornings.

B: Neither do I. It's a right pain, isn't it?

A: But I enjoy school. Lessons are fun.

B: I can't agree. I don't enjoy school – except games.

A: I like reading non-fiction. I like finding out about things.

And so on…

1 Recognise a viewpoint

Getting you thinking

Allow students to express opinions on things they feel strongly about.

Ground rules: No rudeness to others.

How does it work?

Show students, using the examples, that there is often more than one viewpoint on a subject.

Now you try it

Ask students to list the viewpoints they agree with and then the viewpoints they disagree with.

Development

Allow students to write down five viewpoints they agree with and five that disagree with their five viewpoints.

Example:

A carpenter is the best job in the world.

A chef is the best job in the world.

2 Recognise different opinions

Getting you thinking

Model the letter by reading it to the students.

How is it done?

Explain that Desmond Worldwise has strong opinions. Sometimes people express their opinions forcibly. It does not mean their opinions are correct. There is usually an opposite point of view.

Now you try it

Explain to students that the head teacher's reply may not be so opinionated. However, he or she may wish to point out that a) not all children are horrible and b) students at the school wear smart uniform.

Development

Students may wish to see a healthy eating option embedded in the curriculum or a vending machine in the canteen.

Chapter 7 AF7 Relate texts to their social, cultural and historical traditions

STARTER 1

Features of Storytelling

Ask students if they know a good story. The chances are, they do. Students usually know a local legend or two. They might know something that happened to someone near where they live.

Story telling is ancient. People have told stories for years – around campfires, probably in caves. Storytelling is also modern. People tell stories now – in pubs, clubs and in school. People even tell stories in their own homes.

Give this list of tips to students:

To tell a good story, this is what you need to do.

1 Remember, storytelling is an art. It is also 'interactive'. This means you are telling and others are listening and responding.

2 Face the group of people you are telling the story to.

3 Before you start telling your story – wait for silence. Wait until everyone is looking at you. Tell your story as if it is actually happening to you or to someone you know well.

4 If possible, turn down (or turn off) the lights. Try to create an atmosphere.

5 When you begin, let your eyes move slowly around your audience. Keep eye contact all the time you're telling the story. Use your hands and face to show feelings. Use your voice – make sure you can be heard. Change your pace and volume. Don't forget to pause for dramatic effect. Try to begin in a dramatic way. This means you need an exciting start.

6 Keep your listeners interested. Keep them wondering what will happen next. Build up to a dramatic ending.

Example: *(Silence)* … Ohhhh… *(Bang your fists on the table)* …Ahhhhh… *(Dramatic pause)* The arrow buried deep into his chest. *(Dramatic pause)* The king was dead! *(Pause)* The enemy had won. *(Bang on desk three times)* The enemy horses galloped through the ranks of soldiers. *(Dramatic pause)* 'Run, run,' yelled the captain.

1 Recognise stories from the past, the future and other places

Getting you thinking

Allow students to try and work out where the stories are set – in time and place.

How does it work?

Students should be encouraged to look for two clues. For example, in **Story 1** a) campfire, b) young man before the Romans invaded = story set in the past.

In **Story 2** a) Transvaal, b) malaria = story set in a different place.

In **Story 3** a) blue tufts of grass, b) the creatures melted = future/different planet.

Development

Tell students they should put in clues so that their partner can easily guess if the story is set in the past/present/future or in a different place.

2 Recognise local stories

Getting you thinking

With a little prompting, most students know a good local story or two.

How does it work?

Students need to think of a local story, or research one, using local newspapers or the internet.

Now you try it

Allow students to bullet point their stories so that the stories are planned.

Development

Students should practise their stories in small groups before they tell the stories to the class as a whole.